Stress LESS

HOW TO ACHIEVE INNER CALM & RELAXATION

AUBRE ANDRUS

with Karen Bluth, PhD

illustrations by Veronica Collignon

CAPSTONE PRESS
a capstone imprint

Savvy Books are published by Capstone Press,
1710 Roe Crest Drive, North Mankato, Minnesota 56003
www.mycapstone.com

Library of Congress Cataloging-in-Publication Data
is available on the Library of Congress website.

ISBN: 978-1-5157-6822-7 (library binding)

Summary: It can be easy to get bogged down in stress. Luckily there are countless strategies to beat it. When you're feeling anxious or overloaded, the projects in this book can help. Calm down and center yourself with meditation exercises. Boost your mood with a healthy breakfast. Take a break from social media. Relax with some simple yoga poses. Listen to soothing music. Before you know it, you will be less stressed! Your mind — and body — will thank you.

Editor: Eliza Leahy
Designer: Tracy McCabe
Art Director: Kay Fraser
Production Specialist: Tori Abraham

Illustrations by Veronica Collignon, except: Shutterstock: Annykos, 38, runLenarun, 18; **Photographs by** Capstone Studio: Karon Dubke, 39 (both), TJ Thoraldson Digital Photography, 25 (both), 26, 27 (both); Shutterstock: Aleshyn_Andrei, 44, Anastasiya Shylina, 6, Eugenio Marongiu, 32, Fascinadora, 8, Olga Rosi, 34, photolinc, 12 (middle), PhotoMediaGroup, 13, Rica Photography, 28, suriya yapin, 12 (top), violetblue, 16, Vladimir Gjorgiev, 12 (bottom), wavebreakmedia, 10
Design Elements by Capstone and Shutterstock
author photo by Ariel Andrus, 48 (top)

Consultant and contributing author: Karen Bluth, PhD
University of North Carolina, Chapel Hill
Chapel Hill, NC

Printed and bound in the United States of America.
010373F17

Table of Contents

How to Use This Book

Calm. Chill. Composed. Wouldn't you love to feel that way right now? With this book, you can. Really. Because even when you're feeling the exact opposite — stressed out, frustrated, or overwhelmed — there are tips and tricks that can totally transform your mindset and your emotions.

When you're stressed out before a big game, you may get an adrenaline rush that pushes you to focus and gives you a burst of energy. That kind of stress can be good. But chronic stress – stress that lasts for hours, days, or weeks – is harmful.

Thankfully, relaxation can counter the harmful effects of stress, such as feelings of grumpiness and sluggishness and difficulties focusing and remembering. The ideas in this book can help put you in a good mood, make your body stronger, and help you think more clearly.

However, you can't use this book to solve serious mental health problems such as anxiety disorders, depression, or eating disorders. If at any point you think you need more help than this book can offer, please turn to page 44.

IF YOU'RE FEELING TOTALLY OVERWHELMED → LEARN HOW TO MEDITATE ON PAGE 6.

IF YOUR WHOLE BODY FEELS TENSE → TURN TO PAGE 10 FOR MASSAGES YOU CAN GIVE YOURSELF.

IF YOU'RE FREAKING OUT ABOUT TOMORROW'S TEST → TRY THE PROGRESSIVE MUSCLE RELAXATION ON PAGE 16.

IF WORRIES ARE WEIGHING YOU DOWN → TURN TO PAGE 28 FOR A CRAFT THAT CAN HELP.

IF YOU CAN'T DECIDE BETWEEN TWO THINGS → TRY THE DECISION-MAKING TIPS ON PAGE 40.

Meditate

Mindfulness is about being in the present moment with an attitude of curiosity and without judgment. In other words, noticing what you're doing as you're doing it. Breath awareness is a core formal mindfulness practice. It is called a formal practice because you set aside time to do it every day.

Breath and other physical sensations always exist in the present. The more you stay in the present moment, the more you'll let go of stressing about things that may happen in the future or things you might regret about the past. This is why a lot of research has shown that people who practice mindfulness are less depressed, less anxious, and less stressed.

Through feeling the sensation of your breath, you're training your mind to be in the present. Start with 5 minutes and then add a few minutes each day until you're practicing for 20 minutes or more.

- First, find a comfortable place to sit. This can be on a cushion on the floor, or on a chair or couch. If you're sitting on a chair or couch, sit so that your feet are flat on the floor and you're sitting toward the front of the surface, not leaning against the back. Your hands can be relaxed in your lap or on your thighs – whatever is most comfortable for you. Check to make sure your shoulders are relaxed and not hunched. Your eyes can be open or closed. If they're open, keep your lids slightly lowered and pick a place a few feet in front of you on the floor to rest your gaze.

The important thing is that you're sitting in a position where you can be alert. Mindfulness is about observing our moment-to-moment experience, and if we're not aware and alert, we can't do that. We'll just drift away into our thoughts.

- Now bring your attention to your breath in the place where you can most easily notice it. This might be at the tip of your nose as you're breathing in, or at your lips as you're breathing out through your mouth. It might be in the slight rising and falling of your chest as you breathe, or maybe even in your diaphragm area just under your rib cage.

- Feel your breath as you breathe in and as you breathe out. See if you can feel your breath from the very beginning of your in-breath to the very end of your out-breath, even noticing the place where your in-breath turns into your out-breath. Notice the movement of your breath, the temperature of your breath, and maybe even the texture of your breath.

- Do this for each breath, noticing how each breath rises and falls away and noticing the space in between breaths.

- You'll soon be aware that your mind has drifted and you're thinking about something. When you notice this, simply direct your attention back to your breath. No need to judge yourself or feel like you're a "bad meditator." This is what the mind does: It wanders.

- Continue doing this – feeling your breath, noticing that your mind has wandered, and gently guiding your attention back to your breath. Think of your breath like a puppy on a leash. The puppy runs off, and you gently guide it back with the leash. It soon runs off again, and once again you gently guide it back.

That's it! Pretty simple, right? When you are in the moment, you are not dwelling on something that happened in the past or worrying about something that might happen in the future. Research has shown that when our minds wander, they tend to go to these places of worry and regret. So by guiding your attention gently back to the present moment, through paying attention to physical sensations such as your breath, you are letting go of the thought processes that cause stress.

Everyday Mindfulness Practice

Being mindful means being in the present moment with a sense of curiosity and without judgment. There are many ways that you can practice mindfulness "informally" during your day. You can practice mindfulness at any time — while you're walking to class, talking with friends, or playing sports. Since physical sensations (hearing, seeing, touching, smelling, and tasting) always take place in the present moment, these sensations can bring you to the present moment.

Here you will find a few examples of in-the-moment mindfulness practices.

ON YOUR WAY TO SCHOOL

This is a good practice to do if you're riding (not driving) in a car or bus or even walking out in nature. Pay attention to sounds that you hear. Notice sounds that are nearby and sounds that are far away. Notice how they may fade in and then fade away. See how many different sounds you can hear.

Take a minute or two to just listen.

WHEN YOU'RE HAVING LUNCH

Eating is a great time to be mindful. As you are about to take a bite of an apple or raise a potato chip to your mouth, first notice the feeling of the food in your hand. Is it heavy? Light? Smooth? Rough? As you bring the food to your lips, notice if there's an aroma coming from the food. Sometimes it can be very strong, and other times it is subtle. When you bring the food to your lips and take a bite, notice all the sensations in your mouth. Sweet? Salty? Juicy? As you slowly chew, pay attention to the multitude of sensations that are present in your mouth. Notice when that one bite eventually dissolves and is gone. How does it feel in your mouth at that point? Now take another bite, paying attention to the same sensations.

DURING AN ARGUMENT

This practice is very helpful when you feel yourself getting upset. Immediately bring your attention to any place where your body has contact with something solid such as the floor, a chair, or a table. Notice the feeling of your feet on the floor, your legs against the chair, or your hand on the table. Investigate what those physical sensations are like. Is the table cold to your touch? Is the chair hard? You can even bring your awareness to your breath and pay attention to the sensations of your in-breath and out-breath for several slow breaths. This will help keep you in the present and de-escalate any rising negative emotions.

Give Yourself a Massage

Massage therapy is a great way to relax and relieve stress. With the following self-massage strategies, you won't have to go to a spa for an ahh moment. Before you start a massage, gently rub your favorite lotion into your hands. Then sit or lie comfortably in a quiet space.

Mindfulness Tip: As you go through each of these massages, make sure you notice the feeling of tension gently loosening and the area around each part "letting go" a bit. Keep your attention with the sensation.

EYE MASSAGE

Perfect for: soothing tired eyes after a long night of studying or staring at a computer screen.

What you do: Since you'll be massaging around your eyes, don't use lotion on your hands for this massage. With your eyes closed, place your thumbs at the inner corner of each eye socket. Using a small circular movement, softly massage the area. Move slowly toward the end of your eyebrows and back around the bottom of your eye socket until you reach your nose. Repeat several times.

JAW MASSAGE

Perfect for: releasing tension if you clenched your jaw while you slept or during a stressful test.

What you do: Clench your teeth to flex your jaw muscles. Place two fingers directly on each muscle, just below your ears. Now open your mouth slightly while moving your fingers in a circular motion. Repeat for about 30 seconds.

FULL FACE MASSAGE

Perfect for: removing stress from your face at the end of a long day.

What you do: Make fists with your hands. Using your knuckles, trace your jaw from your ears to your chin. Repeat 15 times. Now, with your thumbs pointing down, run your knuckles from the bridge of your nose to the outer corners of your eyes. When you end, your thumbs will be pointing up. Repeat 15 times. Finally, with the thumbs of your fists pointing up, run your knuckles from the center of your forehead to the ends of your eyebrows. Repeat 15 times.

SCALP MASSAGE

Perfect for: releasing tension before bed.

What you do: Don't use lotion on your hands for this massage, since they'll be in contact with your hair. Using your fingers, begin massaging in a circular motion from the back of your head to the front, focusing on the hairline. When you reach your temples, massage in small circular motions, moving toward the center of your head. Continue from the top of the head to the back of the head. Now place your thumbs at the base of your neck and your hands near the top of your head. Massage the base of your neck by moving your thumbs in a circular motion.

HAND MASSAGE

Perfect for: relieving strain from sore fingers after a long day of typing, drawing, writing, or playing an instrument.

What you do: Flex your left hand open and closed a few times. Now take the thumb and pointer finger of your right hand and rub each finger from base to tip. Pull and twist the finger a little as you do. Repeat on the right hand.

FOOT MASSAGE

Perfect for: re-energizing tired feet after a long day of walking, sports practice, or a competition.

What you do: Rest your left foot on your right knee. Holding the left heel with your right hand, use your left hand to squeeze and tug each toe. Now massage and twist each toe. Finally, use the thumbs of both hands to make a strong circular movement on the arch and sole of your foot. Repeat with the right foot.

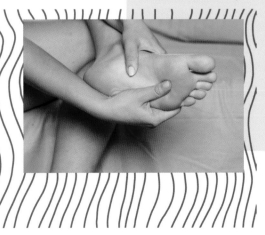

If any of these massages cause pain, stop! Always listen to your body.

NECK MASSAGE

Perfect for: if you slept in an uncomfortable position and wake up feeling sore.

What you do: Place your hands just below the back of your neck and apply pressure with your fingertips. As you slowly pull forward, bend your neck forward for a 10-second stretch. Now wrap your hands lightly around your neck so your fingertips touch the back of your neck, with one hand on each side of your spine. Slide your fingers from the sides of your neck to the tops of your shoulders. Repeat three times. Now slide your fingers up and down the back of your neck. Repeat three times.

SHOULDER MASSAGE

Perfect for: relieving tense shoulder muscles.

What you do: Place your left hand on your right shoulder and squeeze. Slowly rotate the right shoulder backward a few times, then rub your hand up and down your upper arm a few times. Repeat on the other side. Place your left elbow in the right hand, then lightly knock between the neck and right shoulder with your left hand. Repeat on the other side. Using your fingertips, apply pressure to the center of your chest (just under your collar bone) and continue applying pressure as you move your fingers toward your shoulders. Repeat a few times. Finish by making a few circular motions in the same area.

During a massage, you should never apply pressure directly to the spine or the throat.

"WE ASK OURSELVES, WHO AM I TO BE BRILLIANT, GORGEOUS, TALENTED, AND FABULOUS? ACTUALLY, WHO ARE YOU *NOT* TO BE?"
- MARIANNE WILLIAMSON

Tech Detox

There are many reasons why you should step away from technology every now and then. Not only can bright screens disrupt sleep patterns, but social media can also make you feel bad about yourself. When you see a perfectly edited version of someone else's life, it can make you feel as though your life is lacking.

SOCIAL MEDIA ALSO TEMPTS US TO MULTITASK, WHICH IS NEVER AS PRODUCTIVE AS IT SEEMS. IT OFTEN ONLY CAUSES MORE STRESS. YOU MAY BE TEMPTED TO CHECK YOUR PHONE WHILE YOU'RE DOING YOUR HOMEWORK OR EVEN WHILE YOU'RE HANGING OUT WITH FRIENDS OR FAMILY. A TECH DETOX CAN HELP YOU TAKE CONTROL OF YOUR HABITS AND YOUR TIME.

Here are just a few ways to take a tech detox.

ONE-HOUR BREAK

For just one hour, turn off all of your electronic devices, including the TV, and put your phone in a drawer. What will you do with a screen-free, unconnected hour? That's up to you. It might be difficult at first, but rising to the challenge can be so satisfying.

NO TECHNOLOGY AFTER 8:00 P.M.

Starting tonight, make a rule for yourself: "no tech after 8:00 p.m." Find something else to do! Read a magazine, draw a picture, clean your room, play a board game with a sibling or parent, or write a letter to a friend.

TECH-FREE SATURDAY

Feeling a little more freedom? Now that your phone isn't quite so handcuffed to your body, you may be able to take the next step — a whole day without technology. No phone, no Internet, no computer. When you tune back in tomorrow, you'll be surprised to learn that you didn't miss much. Nothing is as urgent as it often seems.

A WEEK OFF

Warning: This is advanced! A weeklong detox is most easily accomplished during a time when school is not in session, such as winter break, spring break, or summer break. If you'd like, you can even give your friends a heads-up — or challenge them to participate! See how many days in a row you can last with no phone, no Internet, and no computer. If you break down, don't completely give up. Start fresh the next day.

"TO LIVE IS THE RAREST THING IN THE WORLD. MOST PEOPLE EXIST, THAT IS ALL." – OSCAR WILDE

Progressive Muscle Relaxation

In this exercise, you'll tense and release as many muscles in your body as you can, starting with your toes and working up to your head.

Be sure to keep breathing steadily throughout these exercises!

DURATION: **WHEN:**
5-10 minutes morning or night

YOU WILL NEED:
a yoga mat, bed, or couch
a quiet space

Directions:

Lie on your back with your arms at your sides and your palms facing up.

Tense your left foot by pointing or flexing it for five seconds, then let the muscles relax for 10 seconds. Repeat with your calf, hamstring, and glutes. Repeat on the right side.

Tense your abdominal muscles for five seconds, then release.

Clench your left hand into a fist for five seconds, then let the muscles relax for 10 seconds. Now tense and relax your bicep, and then your shoulder. Repeat on the right side.

Finish by tensing each part of your face for five seconds, then relaxing for 10 seconds in this order: clench your jaw, smile big, scrunch your nose, squeeze your eyes closed, raise your eyebrows.

SEVERAL STUDIES SHOW THAT THIS EXERCISE CAN REDUCE PULSE RATES, BLOOD PRESSURE, AND RESPIRATION RATES, RESULTING IN LESS STRESS!

Mindfulness Tip: When each muscle is tensed, notice how you're feeling throughout your body. Then with the release of each muscle, notice how the feelings throughout your whole body change.

"THE ONLY PERSON YOU ARE DESTINED TO BECOME IS THE PERSON YOU DECIDE TO BE." – RALPH WALDO EMERSON

Play Mood Music

MUSIC IS POWERFUL

It can get your muscles moving and boost your mood with just a few notes, and it can toy with your emotions in more ways than one. Slow, classical music can soothe your mind, as well as lower your heart rate, blood pressure, and stress levels. Amazing, right? Here are some ideas for music that can change your mood.

MOZART'S STRING QUINTET NO. 5 IN D MAJOR

Some scientists believe in "the Mozart effect": listening to Mozart for 10 minutes before taking a test may help you get a higher score. Other scientists believe any kind of music will give your brain a temporary boost.

Mindfulness Tip: As you listen to the music, pay attention to the sound of each note. When you notice that you're thinking about something and that the music has faded into the background of your mind, gently turn your attention again to the sound of the music. Enjoy each note.

MOVIE SCORES

The instrumental movie soundtrack, or background music, from your favorite movie might be just what you need when you're looking to relax. The soundtracks for *Amélie*, *Grand Budapest Hotel*, *Ever After*, and *Up* are just a few great options.

TCHAIKOVSKY'S BALLET SUITES

Choose from *Swan Lake*, *The Nutcracker*, or *Sleeping Beauty* — all of Pyotr Tchaikovsky's ballet suites are magical. Knowing that someone has danced so gracefully to this music makes you feel lighter than air just listening to it.

"WEIGHTLESS" BY MARCONI UNION

This British band worked with sound therapists to create "the most relaxing song ever." It's eight minutes long, and they don't recommend listening to it while driving. That's how relaxing it is!

WORLD MUSIC

Have you ever tried listening to French jazz? Classic Indian flute? Spanish guitar? Japanese koto music? Every culture around the world creates its own unique sounds. When you listen, you'll feel transported to another place.

ACOUSTIC COVERS

Calming music doesn't have to be instrumental. Acoustic covers of your favorite songs are a great place to start. They're often slower, more mellow versions that are stripped down to just a voice and a guitar or piano.

"WHERE WORDS FAIL, MUSIC SPEAKS."
– HANS CHRISTIAN ANDERSEN

Calming Breakfast Recipes

Breakfast is the first meal of the day, and you might as well start the day with a stress-reducing meal. The following recipes have at least one ingredient that may help you feel ready to tackle the day.

Thank-you notes are the easiest way to express gratitude to a friend or family member. It can be an "I was just thinking about you" note or a special thanks for something in particular, but be sure to end it with a resounding thank you . . . for being a reliable friend, a great mentor, an inspiration, or a source of humor and joy.

Here are some simple ways to say thank you in a card:

- I APPRECIATE YOU SO MUCH.
- YOU MEAN THE WORLD TO ME.
- THANK YOU FOR ALL THAT YOU HAVE DONE FOR ME.
- YOU MADE ME FEEL SPECIAL.
- I'M SO LUCKY TO HAVE A FRIEND LIKE YOU.
- YOU ALWAYS GO ABOVE AND BEYOND.
- I LOOK UP TO YOU.
- YOU HAVE NO IDEA HOW MUCH YOU MEAN TO ME.
- THANK YOU FOR BEING IN MY LIFE.
- I CAN NEVER THANK YOU ENOUGH.
- YOU ARE SO GENEROUS.
- THANK YOU FOR ALWAYS BEING THERE FOR ME.
- YOU READ MY MIND.

- I WILL BE FOREVER GRATEFUL.
- OUR FRIENDSHIP IS A GIFT I WILL ALWAYS TREASURE.
- YOU MADE MY DAY.
- I ADMIRE ALL THAT YOU DO.
- YOU'RE ALWAYS SO THOUGHTFUL.
- YOU HELPED ME MORE THAN YOU KNOW.
- I'M TOUCHED BY THE SUPPORT YOU'VE GIVEN ME.
- YOU'RE THE BEST.
- THANK YOU FOR BEING AWESOME.
- YOU DESERVE MORE THAN JUST A THANK YOU.
- I CHERISH OUR FRIENDSHIP.
- YOU ALWAYS PUT A SMILE ON MY FACE.

Write a card today.

"FEELING GRATITUDE AND NOT EXPRESSING IT IS LIKE WRAPPING A PRESENT AND NOT GIVING IT." – WILLIAM ARTHUR WARD

Strike a (Yoga) Pose

Yoga is about calming your mind and your body. It's a series of poses that involve stretching, balancing, or relaxing. When you're tense, your muscles are tense too. Yoga can help relieve that pressure.

When trying a new pose, focus on your breathing as you move. Don't hold your breath. You can do these poses as a series, one after another, or you can just try one pose when you want to relax. Hold each pose for 30 seconds to one minute.

YOU WILL NEED:

a yoga mat
a comfortable outfit

Triangle Pose

Sanskrit name: Utthita Trikonasana

Step your right foot forward, toes pointing forward. Turn your left foot to a 90-degree angle. Turn your torso sideways. Lift your arms so they are parallel to the ground and in line with your legs. Lean your torso forward, leading with your right hand. When you can't go any farther, bend your body so your right hand touches your leg or the ground. Your left arm and your chin should be pointing straight up. Take a few breaths in this position. Repeat on the other side.

Why this pose is good for you: This twisting pose opens your hips and shoulders, strengthens your back muscles, and can improve your balance with practice.

Wide-Legged Forward Bend

Sanskrit name: Prasarita Padottanasana

Stand with your feet wide apart and your toes facing forward. Breathe in and raise your arms up. Then, with a straight back, breathe out and fold your body slowly forward, letting your arms lower with your body. Touch the floor or grab your elbows and hang your torso upside down for five deep breaths.

Why this pose is good for you: Wide-Legged Forward Bend stretches the backs of your legs and can relieve tension in your neck.

Child's Pose

Sanskrit name: Balasana

Sit up with your knees underneath you. Fold your body forward, slowly sliding your arms directly in front of you until your forehead touches the ground. Take deep breaths as you rest in this position.

Why this pose is good for you: This pose allows your neck and spine to relax while stretching your lower back, hips, and thighs.

Mindfulness Tip: As you're breathing, notice the sensation of your breath as it is moving into your body and out. See if you can stay with the sensation of your breath from the very beginning of each breath to the end of each breath.

Cow and Cat Poses

Sanskrit names: Bitilasana and Marjaryasana

Start on your hands and knees with wrists directly underneath your shoulders and knees underneath your hips. As you inhale, slowly arch your back and turn your gaze forward for Cow Pose. As you exhale, slowly round your back and turn your gaze downward for Cat Pose. Repeat a few times.

Why these poses are good for you: Flowing between these two positions opens your chest, strengthens your abs, and stretches your spine and neck.

Make a Worry Box

Are you a worrywart? If you have a big imagination, a simple worry can turn into an elaborate — and exaggerated — threat. This kind of stress isn't good for your body. Too much worry can have a big effect on your body, from increasing your heart rate to giving you a headache or stomachache.

Here's one way to help lessen the impact of things that are bothering you: store them away! A worry box is a special place to keep your concerns. Simply write down your worry on a slip of paper and then put it in the box. At the end of the month, empty the box and discard all your worries. Or, if you're brave enough, you can read through them. You may find that some of these thoughts took care of themselves . . . and that you had nothing to sweat about!

YOU WILL NEED:

a box
wrapping paper
scissors
tape
stickers (optional)
markers (optional)

Directions:

Use wrapping paper to cover the box as you would with a present. Cut a hole at top of the box. This is where you'll deposit your worries. Decorate with stickers or markers.

Mindfulness Tip: You are free to take them out and look at your worries whenever you want, but having a box for them helps you put them aside so that you don't have to think about them constantly.

"WORRY NEVER ROBS TOMORROW OF ITS SORROW, IT ONLY SAPS TODAY OF ITS JOY." – LEO BUSCAGLIA

Have a Cup of Tea

Teas have great health benefits. Here are just a few that can help calm your mind and soothe your body.

If you don't like the taste of tea, add a spoonful of honey and a drop of lemon juice or milk.

Mindfulness Tip: As you are making and drinking your tea, remember to enjoy the smell of the tea as it brews, the warmth of your teacup in your hand, and the gentle curling of the steam as it leaves your cup. Being mindful of these details can help you find peace.

CHAMOMILE

Some health experts say chamomile helps calm your nerves and helps you fall asleep. Drink a cup an hour before you go to bed.

CINNAMON

The antioxidants in cinnamon could help keep you healthy, and even just *smelling* cinnamon may give you a mental boost.

GREEN

Green tea has an ingredient called theanine that may calm your anxieties and help you relax. But this tea contains caffeine, so don't drink it before bed!

PASSIONFLOWER

Passionflower may help soothe your mind by calming mental activity. That means it could reduce nervousness and may help you fall asleep.

PEPPERMINT

If you have an upset stomach, peppermint can calm the feeling. It can also give you an energy boost that may help keep you focused and confident.

GINGER

Ginger is known for its soothing properties. It can help reduce stress-induced indigestion and alleviate sore, tense muscles.

YERBA MATE

Health experts say this kind of tea offers a balanced energy boost thanks to the caffeine within it. It is said to help overcome both mental and physical fatigue.

LAVENDER

Lavender tea has a calming aroma, and it may help soothe your nerves too. Drink a cup an hour before bed or before a stressful event to help you relax.

"TO LOVE ONESELF IS THE BEGINNING OF A LIFELONG ROMANCE." – OSCAR WILDE

Stop Comparing

When you stop comparing yourself to others, you become happier! Studies have found that self-acceptance is a key element of happiness. That means you accept all the things that make you who you are, knowing that your areas to strengthen are part of what make you human — and what make you interesting. So how do you stop comparing and start loving yourself?

If your social media feeds are making you feel depressed or anxious, delete your account! Or log out for a week and see if you feel any better. See the technology detox tips on pages 14–15 for more ideas.

Mindfulness Tip: Remember that we are all imperfect, because we are all human. Our "imperfections" are what make us who we are.

1. MAKE A LIST OF 10 THINGS THAT MAKE YOU *YOU*.

Writer and director Joss Whedon once said, "Whatever makes you weird is probably your greatest asset." Different is interesting. Whether you're quiet and shy or loud and funny, embrace these qualities. Celebrate yourself!

2. JOT DOWN 10 THINGS YOU WOULD LIKE TO ACHIEVE.

Someone else's path might not be your path, even if it looks perfect from the outside. Any time spent focusing on others is time not spent on yourself. Whatever triggered a jealous response in you is a sign — it signals what you want in your life. Instead of getting depressed about what's missing from your life, look at it as motivation to help you reach your dreams.

3. WRITE DOWN 10 THINGS YOU COULD WORK ON.

Get to know yourself. Instead of avoiding the things you need to work on — such as your tendency to procrastinate on homework — acknowledge them and remember that it's OK not to be perfect. In fact, none of us are. Write down 10 areas you could strengthen. Think about why they are a challenge for you and what you can do to improve these behaviors. Use a kind voice to gently encourage yourself to do your best. Ask a friend or family member for advice.

4. DOCUMENT 10 OF YOUR BIGGEST ACHIEVEMENTS.

So, a friend had something great happen to her lately. It doesn't make all the great things you've done less than. They're still great too! If a friend is smart, it doesn't make you less smart. You can *both* be smart. Being grateful for all the amazing things happening in your life right now will bring you joy. And cheer on others when they have their moment.

> "DON'T COMPARE YOURSELF TO OTHERS. COMPARE YOURSELF
> TO THE PERSON YOU WERE YESTERDAY." – ANONYMOUS

Aromatherapy

Many scientists believe that scents can affect your mood. Imagine the smell of warm chocolate chip cookies right out of the oven, freshly cut grass on a sunny summer morning, or just-washed sheets as you sink into your bed at night.

In aromatherapy, fragrant essential oils are said to naturally influence our mind, body, and spirit. They're not guaranteed to make you feel a certain way, but they definitely smell great. The scents are natural, including lemon, vanilla, or lavender. Sadly, you won't find a chocolate chip cookie essential oil. (Wouldn't that be nice?)

Mindfulness Tip: When you use these essential oils, take a moment to slowly breathe in and really appreciate the aroma.

Here are some commonly used essential oils and their potential benefits:

PEPPERMINT

Energy boosting, invigorating, and promotes concentration.
Good for: when you need to study for a test.

LEMON

Energy boosting, induces alertness, and cleansing.
Good for: when you're feeling run down.

VANILLA

Relaxing, promotes joy and happiness.
Good for: when you want to start your day off right.

LAVENDER

Calming, soothing, and tension relieving.
Good for: when you're feeling stressed.

JASMINE

Revitalizing, confidence inducing, and fatigue fighting.
Good for: when you're feeling blue.

CINNAMON

Mind sharpening, immunity boosting, and tension relieving.
Good for: when you need to focus.

ROSEMARY

Stimulating, pain and anxiety relieving, and clarity inducing.
Good for: when you're exhausted, mentally or physically.

ROMAN CHAMOMILE

Soothing, anxiety relieving, and gentle.
Good for: when you're sore, worn down, or anxious.

ORANGE

Mood-boosting, stimulating, and cleansing.
Good for: when you're disorganized, frustrated, or overwhelmed.

Essential oils should not be used by children under the age of 6. Never apply essential oils directly to your skin. Instead, create one of the projects on page 37 or 39.

You can purchase lotions, candles, and perfumes that are made from your favorite essential oils. Or you can create your own concoctions. Essential oils can be found at health food stores or online.

SCENTED LOTION

Add your favorite essential oil to unscented hand or face lotion, three to six drops per ounce. Be sure to blend well and store in a clean, lidded glass jar. Citrus essential oils (lemon and orange) shouldn't be used on your face or body because they can make your skin more sensitive to the sun.

Try: Peppermint for a cooling effect or rosemary for when you're feeling run down and need a pick-me-up.

FRAGRANT ROOM SPRAYS

Create a room spray or linen spray by adding 15 drops of essential oil to a 3-ounce (89 mL) glass spray bottle. Add 1 teaspoon (5 mL) of witch hazel and top with distilled water. Shake before each use.

Try: Five drops of lavender and 10 drops of Roman chamomile essential oil will create a calming blend that you can spray onto your sheets before bed, or try lemon essential oil for a room spray that could perk you up in the mornings.

SMELLING SALTS

Fill a small, lidded glass jar with coarse sea salt or Epsom salt. Add about 30 drops of essential oil per ounce of salt. When you need a boost, waft the smell toward your nose while breathing in. Replace the lid after each use.

Try: Cinnamon if you need to focus on homework or a test, jasmine for an energy boost, or vanilla when you'd like to calm down.

"IT IS NEVER TOO LATE TO BE WHAT YOU MIGHT HAVE BEEN."
– GEORGE ELIOT

Pamper Yourself

If you're feeling run down, overworked, or stressed out, a little pampering can boost your mood and calm you down. These recipes are a treat for your feet. The peppermint and tea tree essential oils cause a cooling, tingling effect, but they may also put some pep in your step — peppermint is said to be energizing.

YOU WILL NEED:

1 cup (270 g) coarse
   sea salt
½ cup (118 mL) olive oil
12 drops peppermint
   essential oil
12 drops tea tree
   essential oil

Tingly Foot Scrub

After a good massage with this invigorating scrub, your feet will feel soft and smooth.

Directions:

Mix all ingredients in a small bowl.

To use, massage a handful onto your feet while sitting over a bathtub or a large bowl of water with a towel underneath it. Rinse, then pat feet dry with a clean towel. Scoop any extra scrub into a lidded glass container. Store in a cool, dry place. Use within 3-4 weeks.

Be careful. Oils and butters can make bathtub surfaces slippery. A non-slip bath mat may help. Wipe bathtub floor with a dry towel when finished.

YOU WILL NEED:

1 cup (221 g) baking soda
½ cup (125 g) Epsom salts
10 drops peppermint
   essential oil

Foot Soak for Tired Toes

Bring your feet back to life after a long day with this energizing soak.

Directions:

Mix all ingredients in a bowl.

To use, fill a large bowl (big enough to fit both your feet) halfway with warm water. Pour ½ cup (115 g) of the mixture into the large bowl and store the rest in a lidded glass container. Let your feet soak for 10-15 minutes, then pat dry with a clean towel. Discard the liquid in the sink.

Make a Decision

Hit the snooze button or get up? Bagel or eggs for breakfast? These pants or that skirt? Walk or take the bus? Blue or black pen? Every day, you probably make a ton of decisions before the first school bell rings. Sometimes even those little decisions can turn into lengthy internal debates, which can be frustrating.

Major decisions can really wear on you — and on your emotions. The decision-making process is stressful, which makes it hard to think clearly and confidently. Think of a difficult decision you need to make later today or this week. Then try one of these strategies to help you settle on an answer.

When you have to make a choice between two or more things, create a list of criteria that are important to you, then see how many each choice meets.

SET A TIME LIMIT.

Self-imposed deadlines can work for big or small decisions. When you're working against the clock, you'll have to limit the amount of debating, research, and people you talk to for advice. You'll have to eventually go with your gut.

Example: "We'll spend five minutes deciding which movie to watch," or "I'll ask three trusted people for advice on whether or not I should try out for the track team."

MAKE A PRO-CON LIST.

Pro-con lists are especially effective for yes/no questions. To make one, divide a notebook paper into two halves: one for pros and one for cons. Assign one point to each pro and each con. Add up your totals and make a decision based on the results.

Example: "I should join the track team because even though I'll have less free time, I'll make new friends, get in shape, and challenge myself."

LIMIT THE NUMBER OF CHOICES.

Let's say you need to choose a paint color for your room and you have 10 different shades of purple. News flash! You'll never be able to decide. Some of us get so hung up at finding the "best" option that it stops us from making progress. If you have too many choices, quickly reduce the number of options to two or three.

Example: "Let's make this easier: The Freeze or Julie Ann's for ice cream?"

PRETEND YOU'RE GIVING ADVICE TO A FRIEND.

Try to look at the situation from an outside perspective. If a friend came to you asking for advice, what would you tell him or her? If you can separate the decision from your emotions for a few minutes, you might realize there was an obvious choice all along or that you were overlooking some important details.

Example: "When I look at this from an outsider's point of view, I know that I should go because it would be a good experience for me."

CHOOSE YOUR BATTLES.

Is there someone else involved in the decision-making process? Maybe you should just leave it up to that person. If you always fight with your siblings about which movie to watch, you could let your brother choose this one – as long as you get to choose next time.

Example: "I'll let you decide where we eat lunch today, as long as we go to my favorite pizza place next week."

FLIP A COIN.

For smaller decisions, sometimes it's best to leave it up to chance. Assign one outcome to "heads" and one outcome to "tails." Flip the coin in the air and let it land on the ground. Whatever side is facing up is the decision you'll go with.

Example: "Heads means I wear the black shirt, tails means I wear the blue one."

"GO CONFIDENTLY IN THE DIRECTION OF YOUR DREAMS AND LIVE THE LIFE YOU HAVE IMAGINED." – HENRY DAVID THOREAU

Squash Your Stress

Stress balls — or more appropriately anti-stress balls — can help relieve tension one squeeze at a time. Repeated tensing and relaxing of the muscles is a great relaxation strategy. The stress ball helps relieve tense hand and arm muscles and releases energy each time you squeeze. It's also a great way to divert your attention quickly.

YOU WILL NEED:

2 balloons of the same
  color (not blown up)
4-ounce (118 mL) container
  of modeling dough
a permanent marker
scissors

Anti-Stress Ball Craft

Directions:

Cut off the rolled tip at the end of both balloons. Stuff one balloon with modeling dough until the balloon is full. It works best if you stretch the neck of the balloon with two fingers and push a large ball of dough into the balloon. Depending on the size of your balloon, you may not use all of the modeling dough.

Squeeze, roll, and flatten the balloon, holding the open end lightly to make sure no modeling dough escapes, until all air bubbles have been removed. Knot the balloon tightly and trim the excess. Now slide the second balloon over the first to cover the knotted end. Trim the excess. Decorate with permanent markers — a happy face is always a good choice!

Now you can squeeze and squish this ball in your hands whenever you feel anxious, nervous, or scared.

"GREAT MINDS DISCUSS IDEAS; AVERAGE MINDS DISCUSS EVENTS; SMALL MINDS DISCUSS PEOPLE."
– ELEANOR ROOSEVELT

Do You Need Help?

If you've ever thought about harming yourself or others, seek help right away. Turn to page 47 for a list of resources.

The exercises and ideas in this book offer help for short-term stress.

They are not cures or treatments for more serious, long-term issues, such as chronic depression, suicidal thoughts, self-harming behavior, disordered eating, addiction, post-traumatic stress disorder, and generalized anxiety disorder.

Symptoms of more serious mental health issues, such as depression or anxiety, can include any or all of the following:

- LETHARGY AND/OR FATIGUE
- RESTLESSNESS
- FEELINGS OF GUILT
- TROUBLE SLEEPING INCLUDING OVERSLEEPING, INSOMNIA, AND RESTLESS SLEEP
- LACK OF STRENGTH OR ENERGY
- LACK OF INTEREST IN DAILY ACTIVITIES AND HOBBIES
- CHANGES IN APPETITE
- WEIGHT GAIN OR WEIGHT LOSS
- DIFFICULTY CONCENTRATING, MAKING DECISIONS, AND REMEMBERING
- LACK OF SELF-CONFIDENCE
- PERSISTENT FEELING OF SADNESS
- FEELING AS THOUGH YOUR LIFE ISN'T WORTH LIVING
- PERSISTENT PHYSICAL SYMPTOMS IN RESPONSE TO YOUR EMOTIONS (SUCH AS GETTING A HEADACHE OR STOMACHACHE AS A RESULT OF SADNESS OR ANXIETY)

- THOUGHTS OF DEATH OR SUICIDE
- MOOD SWINGS
- SOCIAL ISOLATION OR PERSISTENT FEELINGS OF LONELINESS
- CHANGE IN ENERGY LEVEL
- CHANGE IN SELF-ESTEEM
- FEELING EASILY OR OVERLY IRRITABLE
- FEELINGS OF HOPELESSNESS AND PESSIMISM
- APATHY
- EXCESSIVE CRYING
- SIGNIFICANT CHANGES IN DAILY BEHAVIOR
- LACK OF MOTIVATION
- FEELING "EMPTY"
- SLOWNESS OF ACTIVITY
- RACING THOUGHTS AND/OR EXCESSIVE WORRY
- FEELING A SENSE OF IMPENDING DANGER
- EXCESSIVE SWEATING, TREMBLING, OR SHORTNESS OF BREATH

If any of these negative feelings have been affecting you regularly for two weeks or more, you may need some extra attention. It's important to seek help as soon as possible, especially if your symptoms are affecting your relationships, your health and well-being, or your ability to fulfill your responsibilities.

How to Ask for Help

If you or a friend needs help, there are many people and resources you can turn to. A doctor, social worker, or school counselor can offer professional help. If you need help figuring out how to contact one of these people, reach out to a trusted friend, family member, or teacher.

On a day-to-day basis, friends and family members can keep you on track. Don't forget that asking for help makes you stronger, not weaker.

In addition to seeking out professional help, you can ask supportive, reliable, confident friends and family members to . . .

HELP YOU STAY POSITIVE.

LISTEN WHEN YOU NEED SOMEONE TO TALK TO.

HELP YOU CREATE AND MANAGE A SCHEDULE.

REMIND YOU THAT OTHER PEOPLE STRUGGLE TOO.

MOTIVATE YOU TO FINISH YOUR HOMEWORK ON TIME.

MAKE YOU LAUGH.

HELP YOU GET YOUR CHORES DONE.

PRAISE YOUR PROGRESS.

REMIND YOU THAT YOU WILL FEEL BETTER SOMEDAY.

WAKE YOU UP ON TIME — NO SNOOZE BUTTONS ALLOWED.

GO FOR A WALK WITH YOU.

MAKE DOCTOR APPOINTMENTS FOR YOU.

GIVE YOU PEP TALKS AND TELL YOU WHY YOU'RE GREAT.

WHO CAN HELP

National Suicide Prevention Lifeline
www.sptsusa.org
1-800-273-TALK (8255)

Substance Abuse and Mental Health Services Administration's National Helpline
www.samhsa.gov
1-800-662-HELP (4357)

National Eating Disorders Association
www.nationaleatingdisorders.org
Crisis text line: text "NEDA" to 741741
1-800-931-2237

S.A.F.E. Alternatives
www.selfinjury.com
1-800-DONT-CUT (366-8288)

Gay, Lesbian, Bisexual and Transgender National Hotline
www.glnh.org
1-888-THE-GLNH (843-4564)

The National Center for Grieving Children & Families
www.dougy.org
1-866-775-5683

National Runaway Safeline
www.1800runaway.org
1-800-RUNAWAY (786-2929)

Planned Parenthood
www.plannedparenthood.org/info-for-teens
1-800-230-PLAN (7526)

National Sexual Assault Hotline
www.rainn.org
1-800-656-HOPE (4673)

National Domestic Violence Hotline
www.thehotline.org
1-800-799-SAFE (7233)

National Alliance on Mental Illness
www.nami.org
1-800-950-6264

Read More

Belfield, Annie. *Stressed-Out Girl? Girls Dealing with Feelings*. Berkeley Heights, N.J.: Enslow Publishing, 2014.

Rissman, Rebecca. *Calm Girl: Yoga for Stress Relief*. Yoga for You. North Mankato, Minn.: Capstone Press, 2015.

Woodburn, Judith and Nancy Holyoke. *A Smart Girl's Guide, Worry: How to Feel Less Stressed and Have More Fun*. A Smart Girl's Guide. Middleton, Wis.: American Girl Publishing, 2016.

Internet Sites

Use FactHound to find Internet Sites related to this book.

Visit *www.facthound.com*

Just type in 9781515768227 and go.

Aubre Andrus is an award-winning children's book author with books published by Scholastic, American Girl, and more. She cherishes her time spent as the Lifestyle Editor of *American Girl* magazine where she developed crafts, recipes, and party ideas for girls. When she's not writing, Aubre loves traveling around the world, and some of her favorite places include India, Cambodia, and Japan. She currently lives in Los Angeles with her husband. You can find her website at www.aubreandrus.com.

A mindfulness practitioner for almost 40 years and a lifelong educator, Dr. Karen Bluth is faculty at University of North Carolina at Chapel Hill. Her research focuses on the roles that self-compassion and mindfulness play in promoting well-being in youth. She is author of *The Self-Compassion Workbook for Teens* (New Harbinger Publishers) and co-creator of the curriculum *Making Friends with Yourself: A Mindful Self-Compassion Program for Teens*.